CHRISTIAN APP EMPIRE

How To Spread the Gospel, and Make Money, Through the Lucrative World of Mobile Apps!

SPENCER LONGMORE

Table of Contents

CHAPTER 1 5
INTRODUCTION: WHY MOBILE? 9
CHAPTER 2 13
CHAPTER 3 16
CHAPTER 4 30
CHAPTER 5 36
FINAL WORDS 47
ABOUT THE AUTHOR: 48

DEDICATION:

To my lovely wife and our 3 Princesses.

Copyright © 2015 Christian App Empire LLC

All rights reserved. This book or any portion thereof may not be reproduced or used in any manner whatsoever without the express written permission of the publisher except for the use of brief quotations in a book review.

For more information: www.ChristianAppEmpire.com

CHAPTER 1

Our Story:

Christian App Empire was incorporated in 2014, but was conceived in November of 2013. I became interested in apps after buying my first iPhone earlier that year. It was then that I actually took notice of the world of mobile apps. Prior to that I had a blackberry and hardly ever used apps. However, once I started downloading them, I began to do a survey in my mind about what was out there. Being a creative person, I decided that I should make my own Bible app of the 31 chapters of the book of Proverbs, one for each day. Since this was how I would do my devotional reading: I would read the Proverbs daily along with a passage from the New Testament, given my schedule at that time it was as much as I could do. So having it accessible through an app seemed like it would be a good idea. Now motivated, I ventured out and began searching a little about how to make apps. The first company that I found was Blue Cloud Solutions and basically everything started from there. They had tons of great information, and introduced me to app templates, and since I already had a background in filmmaking, I quickly understood the process that was described to create an app using another source code. I continued with my research and found several other resources out there. Most of what I found, was selling the "Gold Rush" of the app market and in some ways I bought into it. However, the gold rush had already ended in many ways, and the app market was being flooded with new apps daily. However, the best advice that I gathered from them was how to find your niche market and focus on making apps for that specific group of consumers. Most of what I originally got caught up in was making multiple apps, and just putting them out there and if nothing else happens, you at least make some type of money due to the volume of apps I had. In my opinion, this is a good idea for some people if you can handle the load of work involved. However I learned its best to focus on the app voids in your niche, and supplying them with a few quality options for that particular need.

In the end after making over 30 apps, only one of them really came though as a winner. Now I would say that I got lucky because I didn't know it would. Although I knew I had something, I was not certain, which is apart of any business venture, and taking risk.

The risk for me was that I started the business all on debt, with a family of 5 and on an income that was below 30k a year. I would like to note that I don't really recommend starting a business of this type on debt, unless you truly feel led to do so. Additionally, you should be disciplined with your finances and be able to pay the debt off, even if the project is not successful. As a side note, after starting the business on debt, I then heard Mark Cuban, the Shark Tank billionaire shoot down the idea of doing so, and it bothered me and made me think about my decision. However, I realized that it was the best decision for me to make at that time, for many other reasons, than just the possibility of going into more debt. The hard truth for me and my family, and like many others, was that we were already in debt: credit card, student loans, and I was simply searching at the time for something that would help to supplement my income and be a side venture for us.

Furthermore, as I am writing this, I should note that we by God's grace do see the potential of it being so, in the years to come. As this experience has taught me so much about the world of "side businesses," especially online technology based ones. As a result, I now feel 10x more prepared to step into this arena than I ever would have been without first getting started, even if it was on debt. However I advise you, that it took a lot of hard work and continues to do so. Almost 8 thousand dollars later, I will say that the business has lots of potential and we are actually receiving revenue through our apps! So if you think you are going to get into the app market and be a flappy bird's type success, something that I actually tried and thought would happen, since flappy came out while we were about to launch(see Scrappy Dog), remember it's like the lotto, although it is possible, as anything is. I just want to give you a very very transparent overview, which I think the Lord would have me do, so that you don't waste your time or money trying, and I repeat trying to do something that you have no idea about; which is what most smart and determined people are willing to do.

As a result of starting the company, my family was way over our heads in debt, but due to being extremely disciplined with our finances and by His grace, faithful stewards, along with some unwanted government assistance, we were able to survive that time. I am thankful, that we ventured out and started the company. It has pushed my wife and I to new limits and forced us to get out of our comfort zone in so many ways, and shift gears a bit - which can be a healthy way of growing and personally developing. Something I think everyone should be challenged to do, as the Lord leads you.

At the time of writing this - December 2 2015, which is exactly 2 years after starting the company, I have tripled my personal income and the business is actually receiving a monthly side income that is at least enough to pay my family's health insurance, which is not cheap! I say all of this to say that God works in wonderful and very intentional ways, He has a plan for all of our lives, and yes, He has a plan for using our apps to reach and minister to people all around the world. Currently our apps have reached people in over 205 countries with over 1.7million views worldwide, since launching in May 2014. God also had a plan to elevate our family, and this caused us to make some changes and go through some fairly difficult times, but they were necessary and we are grateful for His grace and mercy to get us through!

INTRODUCTION: WHY MOBILE?

In 1982, there were 4.6 billion people in the world but there was not even one mobile phone subscriber. Thirty years later, in 2012, Nielsen reported that smart phones represented over two-thirds of all mobile-phone sales in the U.S. and that 50 percent of all U.S. mobile-phone users—roughly 40 percent of the United States population—uses smart phones. By 2012, the world's population had reached the seven billion mark and the number of mobile phone subscriptions had reached the six billion mark! Of these six billion mobile phone subscriptions, over 70 percent were in the developing world.

In 2012, 17 countries had one telephone line for every two individuals, but 158 countries out of 200 countries that were monitored by the World Bank in that year had passed this threshold thanks to mobile phones. This included countries such as Senegal in West Africa, where the daily average income was only five dollars! The International Telecommunications Union claimed in 2012 that 90 percent of earth's population is covered by 2G networks.

As 2012 came to a close, mobile analytics firm, Flurry, in a post about the rapid increase in time spent inside mobile apps, talked of how mobile devices and apps have made desktop web take a back seat. A few months later, in an April 2013 interview with Christian Post reporter Vincent Funaro, Brent Dusing, Founder and CEO of Lightside, echoed Flurry's sentiments when he was quoted as saying that mobile devices were the fastest growing access points to the World Wide Web. Dusing also said that outside of church, mobile devices were the most prolific method for Christians to enjoy fellowship. The statistics clearly support Dusing's musings about the rise and fall of mobile device use. In December 2014, TomPick revealed that 78 percent of the people who use Facebook, access it through their mobile phones only and that 64 percent of decision makers check their email using mobile devices.

Michael DeGusta, in a 2012 article titled "Are Smart Phones Spreading Faster than Any Technology in Human History?" noted that "squeezed between tablets and ever-smarter phones, the PC is seeing its reign as the world's "personal" computer draw to a close." In August 2014, Catherine Clifford, an *Entrepreneur.com* staff member predicted that 1 billion smartphones would be sold, a number that is double that of personal computers. Even CNN, in 2014, reported that Americans used tablet and smartphone apps more than personal computers to access the world wide web.

Thechurchapp.org provides the following statistics: Americans spend 3 hours a day on smartphones.

Simon Khalaf, in a November 2014 article titled "Mobile to Television: We Interrupt this broadcast (Again)", informs us that more and more, mobile devices are being preferred over television, as America's first screen. The mobile device industry and app industry did not exist a decade ago but the unthinkable has happened. This fledgling industry is replacing the television industry which has been around for the past half century! Michael DeGusta, in the same 2012 article about the spread of smart phones noted that they have outpaced even television in the leap to mainstream use. Smart phones went from a 5 percent penetration to 40 percent penetration in only 4 years, and this was during a recession! The only comparable technology that moved similarly quickly to the American mainstream was television; from 1950 to 1953.

Unlike television screens, mobile devices are portable and are used constantly by the consumers. They have become a part of the daily lives of consumers, even more than television was. Khalaf writes: "All I know is when I am in our living room, I have got a Smartphone on my right, a tablet on my left and a TV remote control somewhere under a couch cushion." The mobile phone habits of millennials are similar to those of Khalaf. In December 2014, Heidi Cohen reported that a whopping 87% of millennials have their smartphone at their side, 24 hours a day, 7 days a week and that 65% of smartphone users in America do check their phones within 15 minutes of waking up in the morning and 64% of smartphone users check their phones within 15 minutes of getting into bed for the night.

An April 2015 report titled "U.S. Smartphone use in 2015" indicated that almost two- thirds of Americans do own a smartphone while 19% of Americans rely on a smartphone for staying connected and for accessing online services. Monica Anderson, in a summary of the same report highlighted the fact that 46 percent of owners of smartphones admitted that their Smartphone was something that "they couldn't live without." Heidi Cohen also reported that 84 percent of teenagers own a mobile phone, while 83 percent of children between the ages of six and nine years old do use a tablet.

Americans spend almost 90% of their time using apps

In March 2015, Khalaf wrote an article about The Phablet. Since the period when phablets became popular, the total time that consumers spent in apps compared to the time they spent in mobile web increased by an extra 2 percent. This increased the total time that consumers in the US spent in apps to 88 percent compared to only 12 percent that they spent on the mobile web.

Massive mobile market due to growth of mobile phones and their ease of accessibility now.

The International Telecommunications Union reported in 2001 that developed countries had six times as many mobile subscriptions as developing countries. Ten years later, the gap had drastically reduced; developed countries had only 50 percent more phones than developing countries. This gap continues to reduce.

A World Trade Organization February 2013 report titled "Electronic Commerce, Development and Small, Medium-sized Enterprises" indicated that between 2011 and 2020, the number of mobile subscriptions in the Middle East and in Africa is predicted to grow at a rate of 5.6 percent each year. This is almost 1.9 percent higher than the global growth average, which is 3.7 percent (page 12).

The same World Trade Organization cites a 2010 report by International Telecommunication Union about the penetration of mobile phones in developing countries. In Africa, the percentage was 45.2 while in South and Central America the percentage was 94.5. Across Asia and the Pacific, the percentage was 69.2, higher than Europe's penetration in 2002 which stood at 67 percent. Comparatively, in 2010, Europe's mobile phone use had grown by only 11.7 percent.

CHAPTER 2

APPS: Market Growth, Downloads and Potential Financial Success

Massive Growth of Mobile Apps Market in the Past 10 years.

TheChurchApp.org notes that Americans use mobile apps three times more than they use mobile websites. According to data from the Adobe Digital Index, a mobile app is a good investment because mobile app users are more loyal to brands compared to those who just visit the brand's website on their mobile devices. Mobile app users use smartphone apps more than twice as often as they visit mobile websites. Use of apps outpaces mobile web visits by about one hundred minutes each month.

In October 2012, 700,000 apps were available for download from Google Play. Six months later, there was a 43 percent increase in the number of apps available for download; the number had reached the 1 million mark. Apple reached 1 million in October of 2013.

Number of Total Mobile Downloads for Android and For IOS.

According to *statista.com* in an article titled "Statistics and facts about Mobile App Usage", by June 2014, over 75 billion mobile software applications (apps) had been downloaded by users, from Apple Appstore. As of June 2015, Apple reported that 100 billion software applications (apps) had been downloaded from the Apple Appstore by users.

Portio Research estimated that the number of yearly downloads would hit the 200 billion mark in 2017. This number is two-and-a-half times more than 2013's 82 billion. Juniper Research forecast that the number of global app downloads would double in the space of four years, rising from 80 billion downloads to 160 billion downloads between 2013 and 2017.

Facts Regarding the Potential Financial Success in the Mobile App Market.

In a "State of Mobile" study of over one thousand software developers, testers, and consumers that was conducted by SmartBear and published in the first half of 2014, it was discovered, among otherthings, that:

- Almost thirty percent of the individuals building apps were building mobile apps

- Thirty percent of registered companies had intentions of developing between five and 20+ new apps in the year 2014.

- Forty percent of app users download between five and 20+ apps in one month.

These statistics show that the app market is growing and will continue to grow, meaning that there are financial benefits to be reaped.

In August 2014, Catherine Clifford, an *Entrepreneur.com* staff member wrote that by

2017, the App Market would be a $77 billion industry, generated by 268 billion app downloads. She pointed out that the mobile app market was already big and that it was just going to get bigger and bigger. Almost half of app users (46 percent) reported to have paid for their apps, meaning that there is a lot of money being made in the app business.

In February 2015, Statista reported that global mobile app store revenues are projected to increase to $76.5 billion by the year 2017. Four months later, in June, eMarketer projected that mobile will overtake desktop for US search ad dollars in 2015, increasing from $8.72 billion to just a little above desktop's $12.82 billion, that is, $12.85 billion. eMarketer also projected that, in the US, the number of mobile phone search users will be 156.4 million, which represents 49 percent of the population.

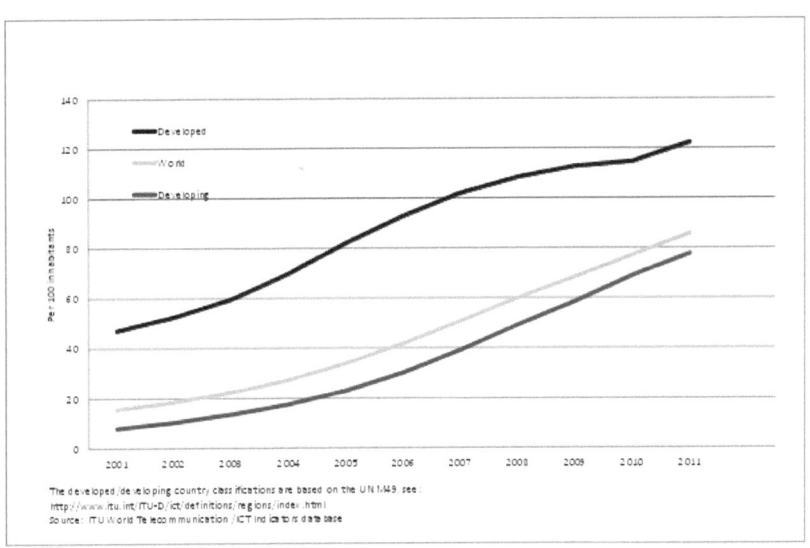

1. Source: ITU - Mobile-cellular subscriptions per 100 inhabitants, 2001-2011

CHAPTER 3

CHRISTIAN MARKET AND TECHNOLOGY

Christians in America and Around the World

In May 2015, Pew Research Centre reported that the number of Americans who profess to be Christians had fallen by eight percent in the space of seven years. In 2007, the number of Americans who identified with Christianity was 78 percent while in 2014, it was 71 percent. However, America is still leading in terms of having the most number of Christians compared to other countries. Second is Brazil followed by Mexico.

Church Attendance in America

An article on *churchleaders.com* highlighted the fact that a 2004 report revealed that less than twenty percent of Americans attended church regularly. This number is half of what other polls reported. A study that was published in 2005 in a reputable journal revealed that the number of people attending church weekly is closer to the 17.7 percent figure given by the 2004 report rather than the 40 percent figure given by other reports.

However, according to a 2008 study by The Barna Group, which has been studying church attendance patterns since the 80s, measuring church participation patterns using attendance at a traditional church service is outdated. This is because Americans are pursuing a growing number of different church options. There are new forms of faith experience and faith communities for example house churches, cyberchurches and marketplace ministries and these new forms must be included in the polls. Millions of Christians are now involved in multi-faceted faith communities. They may attend a traditional church on one

Sunday, go to a house church the next Sunday and interact with an online church community during the week.

According to Barna, a good way of exploring Christians' participation in faith communities is by examining how they practice their corporate faith engagement. Barna came up with five segments namely:

- **The Intermittents** – This segment was composed of people who are under-

    churched. They have participated in a traditional church or faith-based community within the past twelve months but not in the recent month. This segment is made up of 15 percent of Americans, that is, one out of seven adults. Approximately two thirds of people in this group had attended one church event within the previous six months.

- **Homebodies** – These were individuals who had not attended a traditional church service within the previous 30 days but had attended a house church meeting. This segment was made up of 3 percent of Americans.

- **Blenders** – These were adults who had attended both a house church and a traditional church within the previous thirty days. They are the experimenters who although they attend a traditional church as their main church, they are also embracing new forms of faith communities. They represented three percent of the population.

- **Conventionals** – These were the adults who attended a traditional church within the previous thirty days but had not attended a house church. Three out of five adults fit in this category, about 56 percent of the population.

- **The unattached** – Christians who had not attended a traditional church or church community, for example a simple church, a house church or an intentional community within twelve months. Some of these Christians use faith-based media even though they have not had personal interaction with a regular faith- based community. The unattached represented 23 percent of Americans, that is, one out of four adults. A third of this segment was individuals who had not attended a church at all in their life.

Mobile Ministry Opportunities

The Unattached and Unchurched in America

The unattached segment of individuals has an interesting profile. Six out of ten adults in this group identify with the Christian faith. 17 percent of them confessed that they had made a personal commitment to Jesus and had accepted Jesus as their Savior. 19 percent read the Bible and 62 percent prayed. Demographically, they tended to be male, single and divorced at one time or another. This group would be more likely to embrace Christian content delivered to their mobile phone through Christian apps.

George Barna, in his book, "Grow Your Church from the Outside," described the unchurched in the following way: "those who live without a regular face-to-face faith connection tend to be relatively isolated from the mainstream of society, tend to be non- committal in institutional and personal relationships, and typically revel in their independence." The mobile phone is a tool that would let them keep their independence but at the same time continue to feed them with the Gospel.

Introverts

Introverted Vinay Kumar, in a July 2010 article titled "How Introverts are Finding Their Way in Associations" wrote of how online social networking tools were giving introverts a comfortable method of expressing themselves and connecting with their communities. Mobile phones, smart phones and apps can do a lot to reach this segment of Christians who often feel out of place in the usually highly extroverted church setting. As Kumar asks in the article: "In today's 100-mile-per-hour, extroverted culture, to what degree are introverts overlooked and misunderstood?"

The questions that Kumar asks about a statement made by an association membership director apply to church leaders. Are churches "more friendly to those members who are more comfortable with, and thus prefer, face-to-face communication? If so, what happens to those who are more reserved, preferring other means of interacting and communicating?"

Speaking of his introverted personality and tendencies, Kumar gives us an insight into the characteristics of an introvert: "At meetings I sit back, I listen to various views, and only then do I speak. From my perspective, I am listening at a deep level, being thorough, diplomatic, precise, and an "anchor of reality," working toward making good decisions so everyone's benefits." He then points out that "New technologies are allowing a broader spectrum of our members to engage, particularly introverts." However, the encouragement to these types of believers is to remind them of the benefits that God has blessed us with through direct in person community and fellowship. As we are in fact commanded in scripture to do so (Acts 2:42; Hebrews 10:25).

Foreigners

Evangelizing in foreign countries is a costly (both in terms of time and money) and often dangerous endeavor. However, with mobile phones, the cost and the danger can be drastically reduced while having the same or even greater impact. There is a huge opportunity for the use of mobile phones for taking the Gospel to the ends of the world. According to the same World Trade Organization report mentioned above, the most popular ICT in countries which are still developing, and one which is progressing at a very fast rate in both Asia, Africa and India is the mobile phone.

Christian Apps Demand vs Supply

The Christian market – both locally and globally - is underrepresented in technology, especially in the arena of mobile apps. There aren't many apps that are specific to Christians for everyday use. To underscore this fact, let us explore some of the technology products available for the Christian market.

2012

World's First Christian Tablet

Brian Honorable, a technology supervisor at Family Christian, the organization that sells the tablet was quoted as saying that the organization wanted to offer their customers the ability to utilize the organization's Holy Bible application. The application has over two dozen English translations of the Bible. Honorable went on to say that the organization wanted to reach people with the Word of God through the tablet.

Software/Apps

Logos5 and Olive Tree released in the second half of 2012.

Olive Tree Bible Study App - The mission of Olive Tree is to inspire people to connect with God and the Bible through technology. More than 4 million people in six continents use this app.

TheGreatCommissionMobileApp

In July 2012, Christian Apps Ministry developed an evangelistic mobile app that leveraged social media to share the Good News. The app provided user-friendly and non-confrontational tools for evangelism, especially to individuals who have a Buddhist, Hindu or Muslim worldview. The app used Email, Twitter and Facebook to spread the Gospel to friends, family, coworkers, neighbors and even strangers via a "Why Christianity" audio message link. The app also assists people to find a Bible-based church near them via GPS or by entering the address zip code.

Apps for busy Christians

The 21st century pace of life is hectic and frenetic and even Christians are not spared from the busyness of life. However, as Christians, busyness is no reason to fall behind on feeding your spirit with the things of God. Luckily, technology has provided a way for Christians to feed their spirits in the midst of a hectic life. Below are some of the apps that are designed to keep the busy Christian spiritually nourished even in the midst of a frenetic life.

- NRT Weekly

This free app, available for iPad and iPhone gives dynamic and real-time inspiration through the latest Christian music. If you are a fan of *Newreleasetuesday.com*, then you will like this app because it gives you access to the most recent music releases and music videos. Furthermore, this app will give you inspiration from the various artists themselves via the interviews. The app allows you to bookmark your favorite interviews and songs so that you can share them with your friends and family or so that you can listen to them anytime you need some inspiration.

- Proverbs in a Month

This free app from iPhone will give you access to the whole book of Proverbs. You can read one chapter every day for thirty one days. This app will bookmark where you stopped reading so that you can continue from where you left off. The proverbs are set in an appealing way, on a relevant motivational photograph every day.

- iChristian Circle

This app (free for Android) provides a wonderful support system. You can seek advice from other Christians, you can share prayer requests and you can even use it to keep a journal of your daily walk with Christ.

- Church Signs

This app is available for iPhone at just under 2 dollars. It spreads the Word of God via an eye-catching collection of motivational signs shot from all over the United States at a variety of Church locations.

- Daily Broadcast

This Focus on the Family app that is free for Android gives a daily dose of encouragement and advice, with emphasis on the family. You can listen to anecdotes and inspirational topics from Jon Daly, John Filer and Dr. Julie Slatery. The app focuses on marriage, parenting, relationships and the responsibilities of Christians in the society.

- DVO- Christian daily devotion app

This app features Bible verses that will inspire your prayer walk. The apps, written and designed by Pocket Fuel, deliver Bible verses to you every day. One user of this app wrote a review saying that the app changed her life because she used to slack off reading the Bible and praying. However, it helped her to get back on track, despite being very busy with school and reminds her to read the Bible. Another user compliments the app's visual appeal as he is a very visual person.

Proverbs 31 App

"Who can find a virtuous woman? Her price is far above rubies."-Proverbs 31:10

Are you a Christian woman looking for a Christian-themed app that will motivate and inspire you? Well, look no further than the Proverbs 31 app created by Christian App Empire. The app focuses on the thirty-first chapter of the book of Proverbs which outlines the attributes of a virtuous woman.

The thirty first chapter of Proverbs advises Christian women to work ("She seeks wool, and flax, and works willingly with her hands"), to guard the hearts of their husbands,"The heart of her husband safely trusts in her" and to fear the Lord "Favor is deceitful, and beauty is vain; but a woman who fears the Lord, she shall be praised."

The Proverbs 31 app gives a daily verse and will enable you to record your favorite ones, then listen to them on playback mode all through the day. The app also allows you to memorize the verses you like, to save the recording and to share them with your family and friends via sms or on social media. One of the screenshots of the app shows a verse from the book of Ephesians, chapter five verse twenty-five which says "Husbands, love your wives, even as Christ also loved the Church, and gave himself for it."

Christian Colleges Adopt Mobile Apps

Top Christian colleges have adopted mobile applications to aid their stakeholders in various college-related activities. Below are some of the mobile apps beings used by Christian Colleges in the United States,

iMessiah

This is Messiah College's mobile app. It puts key information at the user's fingertips without the user ever having to leave his or her home. The user can take a tour of the Messiah College Campus, schedule a visit to Messiah College and can even apply to join the college directly from his or her smartphone.

CUMobile

Cedarville University's mobile app allows one to view the university's calendar, to find various people to browse the classifieds, to read the campus news and to check one's transfer meal count at the dining hall. This app also allows the user to view the campus map and building list.

Ellucian GO app

The Ellucian GO app of Union University provides users with free and convenient access to Union University's information and services. This app is integrated with two of Union University's major information systems, namely the Moodlerons course system and the Ellucian Colleague Student Database.

The Pensacola Christian College Web app

This app features a calendar that lists daily events such as the times of the Planetarium show and the Eagle sports competitions. The app also features a News and Events section where the user can read various articles about both past campus events and upcoming campus events. With this app, you can follow the Eagles' team schedules and also keep track of the game results. You can also access the team roster to find out more about the players.

The Pensacola Christian College Web app also allows you to view the dining menus for each of the meals, all week long. Additionally, the app has a Spotlight's section where you can read different articles about the graduates of the college and their views on how the college's training has benefited their careers and their ministries. Also included in the app are the Palms Grille menu and the college's various Twitter accounts.

Anderson University Mobile app

This app was launched in May 10, 2011, making Anderson University the very first Midwestern University to provide web accessibility via an app. The app features news, events, admission information, academic programs, "going to AU" and many other features.

2014

Righteous Tales: David Vs. Goliath

In July 2014, Christian Post reporter, Vincent Funaro wrote an article about an iOS App that tells the famous David and Goliath Bible story in a new engaging way. The App was created by Gerald Hinsen, a former employee of Microsoft. Hinson told The Christian Post that: "Youth Pastors have a pretty rough job. Once a week they are trying to relate these Bible stories to 50 to 100 kids at a time and you're also trying to breach cultural divides. And I thought it would be cool if there was some [quality resources] that we could hand the kids after service. [I asked] why don't we have quality versions of these stories for these kids devices that they are carrying around all the time."

Although there were similar apps in the market, none of them delved deeply into the Bible stories. In Hinsen's App, they took time to explore the characters' personalities. For example: "When Merab, the daughter of King Saul is being offered as part of the prize for the person that kills Goliath, we put her in the scene and she's standing there in front the soldiers and they're kind of oodling and we [asked] what was she thinking. She probably resented it. So we kind of portrayed her as teenager that's not at all impressed with her dad."

In 2015, on *geero.net*, the writer who is a Christian developer, met Gerald Hinsen. Regarding the David vs Goliath app, he wrote that Gerald Hinson had "never done anything like it before, but he saw a need, saw how God had given him the talents and the connections and the passion to make it possible, and he made it happen, despite all the challenges and an awful lot of hard work along the way."

Gerald Hinson seemed to have created this game "as unto the Lord", if the review by one Andy Geers is to go by. Geers wrote in July 2014 that: "One of the standout features of this game is the sheer quality of the graphics and animation. The game looks gorgeous. The animation is beautifully done and really adds to the humor of the story. I don't know a lot about the team behind the game, but they clearly know what they are doing."

2015

In a 2015 article titled "The World Map of Christian Apps: 48 tools every Christian should know", Jeffrey Kranz gave a comprehensive list of some of the Christian Apps available. However, not all of the "apps" are mobile-based. Below are some of the mobile-based apps highlighted in the list. These apps are both faith and family centered:

- The Bible App by YouVersion (free), has been downloaded more than 100 million times.

- Bible.is features text, video and audio Bibles in over 1600 languages including several international sign languages. Claims to have the world's largest Bible language library.

- Bible Gateway

- Bible Web App – developed by Digital Bible Society.

- Bible memory apps – for scripture memorization.

- Fighter Verses – This scripture memorization app comes preloaded with not one but two, five-year memory plans.

- Sharefaith Presenter – This is a powerpoint plugin which builds the features that a church needs right into PowerPoint. According to their website, almost 90 percent of churches utilize PowerPoint so they just re-invented PowerPoint via a powerful worship software plugin. This app lets the user add text over any video. It also allows the user to build countdown timers and access the most extensive database of worship lyrics. The user can also add scripture from the in-built ESV and NLT database.

- Proclaim is targeted to pastors and other leaders who frequently deliver sermons.

- Christianity Today – News from the Christian world in app form.

- Bible Pathway Adventures – An engaging Bible storybook app which helps parents and guardians to teach their children about God and God's Word. The Bible stories are interactive and explore the historical context of each story, including archeological facts.

- Bible for Kids app – Has interactive and illustrated Bible stories.

- Superbook – This app complements the much-loved Emmy nominated Christian Broadcasting Network series of the same name.

- Adventure Bible Memory – iPhone App for children.

- Bible Coloring Book – a coloring book app.

- PrayerMate – Helps the user to keep track of prayer requests.

- Prayer Calendar – Helps the user to remember persecuted Christians throughout the world. It also alerts the user to specific prayer requests every day.

- Praying God's Word – An "app-ccompaniment" to the best selling book of the same name, written by Beth Moore.

- Daily Bible Inspirations

- The Church App platform enables churches and ministries to create their own high quality mobile apps. Utilizing the easy to use online App Builder, churches can control content, layout, features, themes, and artwork in real time.

CHAPTER 4

APP DEVELOPMENT AND ADVERTISEMENTS

Ads and Apps

Many people, including Christians, do not like advertisements when they are using their mobile phones or smart phones. But advertisements are a necessary evil and they are here to stay. However, Christian app developers need to find more creative and less intrusive ways of creating apps that feature advertisements. Christian app developers should know whether the app is intended for ministry or for business. Either way, there should always be the option of buying the app with no ads or have the option of removing the ads for a nominal fee.

Sunil Gupta, in a 2013 article titled "For Mobile Devices, Think Apps, Not Ads", suggested that the most effective way for marketers to communicate through mobile will be via apps, mainly because users do not yet perceive apps as advertising. Apps are valued for their functionality and therefore consumers do not find them intrusive like other forms of advertising. Marketers, including those in the Christian community such as Churches, Christian Universities and Christian businesses, should also adopt apps for advertising because they are more cost-efficient than traditional methods of advertising. Also, they can create new revenue streams.

App Reskinning or Flipping

App flipping is the process through which app developers can create a positive Return on Investment on an app or app framework that already exists. It is the way you add value to an app. Any app that has Christian themes or that helps a Christian grow in his or her faith obviously is of value to him or her. It is a fact that app stores do not provide a lot of Christian apps. This is a big opportunity for Christian app developers. They can use what is already available and popular in the app market and then customize it to be of value to Christians all over the world.

App <u>reskinning</u> can be your biggest passive income opportunity. The necessary skills and hardwork are required but the benefits are definitely worth it. The aim of reskinning is not to duplicate apps but to reach new audiences by simply changing the themes and appearances of existing apps. Reskinning would work well in a Christian context because Christianity has a clear and definite set of rules and guidelines that apply to every situation a Christian finds themselves in. This means existing apps can be reskinned to have Christian themes.

If you already have a successful app, you can introduce the sequel with minimum improvements, new graphics and the all-important "2" in the app's title! In the case of Christians, an existing app can be reskinned to be the Christian version. Perhaps a Christian version of Angry Birds? Which we actually developed called *Sling Shot Sheep*. Which is the same concept just using sheep, and a sling shot to toss them across the screen. The point is that Christian app developers can use what is already popular and customize it for the Christian community. Alternatively, Christian developers can make a free app, and a PRO version. Also you can use in-app purchases to remove ads, or have one app with no ads that is your paid version, and one with ads that is your free verison.

Flipping high-growth market apps for the Christian Market

Andy Patrizio, in January 2014, wrote an article about making money in mobile app development by targeting high-growth markets. He listed the following high-growth markets:

- Fitness
- Concierge apps
- Game-changers
- HTML5

Let us look at how Christian app developers can flip existing apps or develop new apps in the first two areas, namely, Fitness apps and Concierge apps.

Fitness

The market research company called HIS iSuppli predicted that global installations of fitness and health applications will grow by 63 percent from the year 2012 to 2017. A consumer survey by the same organization revealed that 62 percent of the respondents wanted to use fitness and sports apps and were prepared to buy hardware that increases the functionality of the software. Shane Walker, then a senior manager at HIS pointed out that:"Sports and fitness apps have become an integral part in the daily lives of millions of mobile users, allowing them to use their smartphones to do everything from tracking running distances, to recording their strength training sessions, to monitoring their heart rates,"

Christian fitness and sports apps can be flipped or developed for the Christian market. They could include features such as:

- encouraging Bible verses to encourage overall health and fitness like; 1 Corinthians 10:31 "Therefore, whether you eat or drink, or whatever you do, do all to the glory of God." And "1 Corinthians 6:19-20 "Or do you not know that your body is the temple of the Holy Spirit who is in you, whom you have from God, and you are not your own? For you were bought at a price; therefore glorify God in your body and in your spirit, which are God's."

- And Galatians 5:16 "I say then: Walk in the Spirit, and you shall not fulfill the lust of the flesh." The lust of the flesh includes: selfishness, lack of self-control and drunkenness. Another verse is: Proverbs 23:2 "And put a knife to your throat if you are a man given to appetite."

- Also Corinthians 9:27 "But I discipline my body and bring it into subjection, lest when I have preached to others I myself should become disqualified.

- A training/work out playlist featuring fast, upbeat Christian praise and worship songs such as Crystal Lewis's remix of the popular Christian song "Shine Jesus Shine". Or "Undignified" by David Crowder Band/ the Hindi version by Sheldan Bengara. Or playlists courtesy of *spiritfitmusic.com*

- We have as a result of this advice created our own fitness apps, called **Proverbs 31 Fitness** and **Christian Fitness: 30 Daily Inspirational Challenges**

Concierge apps

Concierge apps are the ones that assist people to do things. For example travel apps help people to book flights, hotel rooms, cars and dinner. They help travelers to find out when planes are arriving and puts their travel itinerary in one place. These are the most popular apps in Google Play and App Store. These are the apps that people, such as business travelers are willing to pay for. Furthermore, they involve a lot of coding and development, so although it's a popular niche, reskinning an app like this can be very expensive, and I personally wouldn't recommend doing it.

Christian developers can flip existing apps to cater for the Christian market. These apps could include Bible verses about travelling/protection while travelling. Which is not so much a concierge app, but you can in fact theme an app for people traveling. For example, Luke 4:10 'He will put his angels in charge of you to watch over you carefully." Psalm 91:11 For he will command his angels concerning you to guard you in all your ways. Psalm 91:4-5 He will cover you with his feathers, and under his wings you will find refuge. His truth is your shield and armor. You do not need to fear terrors of the night, arrows that fly during the day

Christian app developers should also identify particular problems in the Christian community then make an app that provides a solution.

Recent App Developments

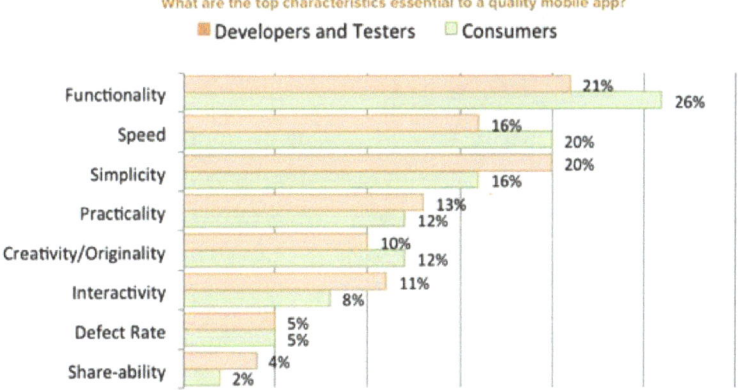

A slide from SmartBear's State of Mobile 2014 webinar and eBook

If you would like to read the "Thoughts of a Christian Software Developer" then *geero.net* is the website to visit. In October 2015, 800 Christian developers and designers participated in a global hackathon titled "Code for the Kingdom" .Some of the London app projects included:

- Flee! – a low-touch accountability app that pings appropriate Bible verses when it spots the user typing inappropriate web URLs

- Let's pray for… – a prototype for a fantastic social prayer app, that I really hope comes to life soon!

- Verse of the day – Microsoft Band app to give you a verse each day

CHAPTER 5

CONCLUSION

"We live in a world that is so lost and confused when it comes to knowing God– and nowhere is that more obvious than on the Internet!" These are the thoughts of a Christian developer on *geero.net*. He goes on to write that modern technology offers an incredible opportunity for getting the gospel out there and to further the work of the kingdom of God. He points out that for many Christian organizations such as church plants and charities, the number one limiting factor is having the right people to design and develop the tools for turning an idea into a useable product.

Like former Microsoft employee Gerald Hinson, Christian developers need to get more involved in Christian game and app development. The market is there, the tools are there and the Gospel is there, ready to be taken to the ends of the world via mobile phones, smartphones and tablets. The field is ripe for harvest and the current tools that can be used to bring in the harvest is in the form of apps and mobile technology. These new technologies and devices will also allow for a broader spectrum of church members to engage, including the usually marginalized introverts.

Apple, Android and Amazon markets are now global, meaning that the Gospel of Jesus Christ can be shared directly with people from all over the world, on a daily basis, right through their phones. Churches will be able to better reach their members and non- members with their message, both locally and globally. As Keith Williams pointed out in the 2012 Mobile Ministry Forum: "Never before in human history has there been a technology as highly personal, rapidly deployed, and universally embraced as the mobile device...[it] represents the most important technology available for kingdom advancement."

There is no doubt that there are great opportunities and enormous potential in the market for Christian apps. The preceding chapters gave you the opinions of many developers who are currently working in that field, statistics and a general overview of the Christian app marketplace in America and worldwide.

Furthermore, here is a step-by-step guide to get you started in pursuing your dreams and desires of developing your first mobile app:

Step-By-Step Guide To Help Get You Started:

- ***Think of problems and voids in the Christian market.***

I thought there weren't enough quality Christian themed games. There still isn't. However, please note that I now understand that to compete in the game market it takes many marketing dollars, even a modest budget, just to get the word out. Games are not the easiest field to burst into success with, although many of the app developers selling programs and eBooks on how to make them will say that games are the best place to start.

For the Christian market I learned that when it comes to apps, most Christian kids are just playing secular games that their parents deem as clean. Most Christian parents don't actually go on the app store and look for Christian games, it's the kids who come to the parents and say "mom can you buy me this or is this okay for me to download" etc.? Now most kids of Christian families are not saved, so why would they look up Christian games? Unless prompted by an advertisement or their parents. This is just my thought given my experience, no real research but it is something to consider. I won't say not to make games, I have 10 of them out there, and organically speaking they have not done well. That means just from general searches alone, and no marketing, they have not had much downloads.

- ***Once you find your problem or that void in the app market then I would say to start coming up with your own ideas. Then I would start looking for a template. Here is what I did.***

I wanted to make a text only app. So I looked up quotes app templates. I found one but it was too expensive for me. Then in that same process I found, *Odesk* which is a website for freelancers, and its now merge with another called *Elance*, who changed their name to *Upwork*. I posted a job on their for a developer to make this type of app and I found someone to do it for $18. Now he made the entire app from scratch. It was a very basic app, and the reason why he did it for so cheap, is because he was trying to get reviews on his account, so he could start getting more jobs, as he was new on the site.

This has been my strategy, however I will warn you, that when working with developer's overseas, for a low cost, you are taking a risk. However, once you get the hang of it, you will be able to discern fairly quickly, if they can speak fluent English, have a solid resume, and answers your questions in a way that provides you with the needed confidence to begin working with them.

Note: I only work with developers at a low rate once or twice, as they will move on and raise their rates, which is understandable. The bad thing about that is if you want to update your app, it will be easier to just go back to them, but it will cost you and they know it. So try to build a good relationship with them and they will help you out, at a much higher but better rate.

- *After getting your template or source code you will need to figure out what you want the app to look like.*

Therefore, you will need to design the app, but this design is based on what you will be changing from the template you already see and are using as the base. So you might start with your idea, find a good name for it, which should also be in conjunction with your market and what problem your're trying to solve. Example, I thought there weren't enough games, so I made a game based on the 80's "Simon Says" game called "Jesus Says-Follow the Light."

The game made you follow around the light in a circle with different colors. As this is how you have to think when using a template. I then gave that idea to my designer, whom I hired on *Elance*, and he then presented me with his first take on it. This was my very first time receiving a design back from a designer for an app, and to be honest I was super excited, and encouraged by the possibilities.

Afterwards I gave him back several notes and he continued to submit his ideas, until we finalized the project. After using *Elance* I realized that I paid a premium although his work was really good, I moved on to *Odesk* and another website called *Fiverr*, where you guessed it, everything starts at a price of $5! You are working with freelancers from all parts of the world, doing all different types of jobs. I found everything from someone to write my app description to someone to make my app icons! Take a look at my first mobile app designs below:

Version 1

Version 2

Final Version

- *After you have bought or developed your template you now need to test your app.*

This part is fun, and it's about you getting a feel for what you have created. My advice is to let other people see it and test it also. Get their feedback and take notes, and send them to the developer. The developer should send you a revision or updated draft, test and repeat those steps.

- ***The next step is to upload your app.***

I started with Apple because I had an iPhone, but you can start with Android if you have that type of phone. I would say start on either one, it just depends on your preference, and goals. There is more research to be done as to why you would start on either one, which I would advise you to Google. However my reason for using Apple is simply because I was using that kind of phone, and it was easier for me to test the apps, plus I had actually bought an apple computer to do so.

- ***Once the app is uploaded you now have to wait on Apple to get approved.***

This process can be anywhere from 1-2 weeks. For Androids it usually takes about one day and there is no real approval process, unlike with Apple.

- ***Once your app is live on the App Market!***

Go out and tell everyone you know to download it, or people you know who are relevant to your apps market. You can also promote your app on Google and Apple advertising platforms known as iAds for Apple and Admob for Google. If you implemented ads in your app then you would have had to learn about the ad networks. I chose to use Admob from Google and iAds from Apple. This just made it simple for me to understand since I was making apps on both these platforms. They also have back cpanels that sort of navigates you to each of these areas, so it was just convenient for me to start this way. I only work with these two networks now, but when I started out, I was testing and or using Revmob and Chartboost. These were recommended by many different app developer "guru's" out there. I put those ads in my game apps and to be honest have not made any money from them. Does that mean they are not effective or good options? No - I'm just telling you my experience. My general advice is to please do your research on ad networks for promoting your apps and for monetizing your apps.

- ***Also you will need to figure out if you want to start a business or just use your personal name to promote your apps on the app market.***

Starting a business means you have to prove you are one. This means that you should have an incorporation number available, or you can just use your name and assume the liability to avoid those other steps. I chose to start a business, for the protection because I did not know exactly what I was getting into and I knew it would just be safer in the long run for my family and I. It was also easier to track and separate from my personal and family finances. Is there a benefit to doing either or on the app markets? Not really- it's a preference from a more business perspective. I don't think that part has anything to do with the actual app market and being able to be more successful or not. I don't believe anyone downloads apps simply because it has a business name or not. They might find you on the app market because of a name though, if its common and catchy. However, if your app is hot and your company name is Cookie Polka Dot, no one will care!

- ***Last but not least, I released my apps and did not get the response that I was looking for and I honestly wanted to give up!***

I was done, I just wanted to never look at an app again and I didn't for a few months, and when I came back to it, things were moving along. But I didn't quit, the Lord by His grace put a burden on my heart through the 100's of reviewers and thousands of downloads the apps were getting. So I felt obligated to respond and tend to what the Lord had put me in charge of and not abandon it. Let me advise you that I come from a culture of "need things to happen like yesterday" the quick fix, and if it don't hit, I don't want nothing to do with it!

It's just a mentality that doesn't allow you to stick through with things or even have a long term preserving vision in your mind, understanding that everything takes time. Nothing, and I mean nothing is successful overnight. Its extremely rare.

With that being said, I will leave you with what the Lord says, that in the end it is His Word that shall remain, and that which He has prepared us to do for good works. So if you are blessed with the ability and opportunity to make an app for the kingdom and release it, then see it through.

You don't know what the Lord has planned for it, and it's your duty to wait it out to see. Whatever you do, enjoy and respect the process along the way, and understand that if you are reading this with the genuine hope of making apps, that you are blessed. There are many who not only can't read, but don't even have the means or ability to fathom making an app. Most people look at their phones daily and the thought does not ever even cross their minds(*that included me*), about making an app or let alone putting in the time to actually get one onto the market.

Many experts and statics, claim that apps are the way of the future, well to be honest we are living that future, and most people will be consumers of apps, not developers. So I encourage you, as there is a baby born every day, I venture to say this is true for believers in Jesus, that there is a Christian born every day! So remember as the Lord said the harvest is plenty and the laborers (developers) are few...in the world of Christian Apps!

What About Developing Apps from Scratch:

This is something I only recommend if you either have the money to invest or you are making something very simple like a text based app. Similar to our Proverbs 31 app, which is mainly just text content, and its not a game or utility app etc.

Otherwise I would buy a source code. The places I bought my source codes from were, Code Canyon (Envato), and Apptopia, but there are many others out there nowadays, where you can get quality source codes. Furthermore, there are other basic apps out there that don't take much time or money to make from scratch. This I recommend doing if you want to learn the process of creating from scratch, or want to own your source code and won't have to buy a license from another developer.

The licenses sometimes are limited or they cost more money than it would probably cost to make the same basic app from scratch. That is my thought on developing from scratch, which I find myself doing mainly for Android apps, more than for IOS, as Android development is generally cheap or more affordable. However, it is easier to modify source codes for IOS than for Android.

So if I want an Android version of my app I generally have to get it made from scratch. If it's not being made from scratch I probably would get an app that functions similarly but not exactly and just name it the same as the IOS version.

In the end if you want to create an app like Instagram or Facebook, then starting from a template someone has made, to test your idea, is a good way to go, since making an app like that can be a extremely pricey undertaking if you are not a developer.

Although once you have tested and want to move forward with that size of an app, you would want to start over from scratch, just so you understand and know each part of the code, and that it is 100% yours. Allowing you the ability to make as many modifications, as you like with no restrictions. Now if you are like me and just want to make unique niche market apps, whether or not you want to develop from scratch or use a template, will simply come down to preference.

FINAL WORDS

So often we can get into this field thinking that it's about an app, but really I have learned that it's about the journey and how you respond to the things God is doing in your life along the way. He cares about our heart's attitude, and making us more like Jesus, than about us just trying to make an app, whether the app is for Christians or not.

Therefore, please keep in mind that as you push forward in your endeavors and pursuits, that you consider God's will in all that you are doing. Hearing from Him and seeing where he is pointing you to bring your gifts and talents, for people through mobile app creation and what that app would be. In conclusion, I pray that my story can help you on your journey of developing apps for God's glory!

FURTHER READING **https://www.cmocouncil.org/facts-stats-categories.php?view=all&category=mobile-marketing**

ABOUT THE AUTHOR:

Spencer Longmore born in Harlem, N.Y, and raised in the South Bronx, NY, is a faithful husband and father who lives in Los Angeles, California, with his wife and 3 kids. He loves Jesus, filmmaking, and spending time with his family and friends. He also enjoys watching Tennis(*Serena Williams mostly* ☺), playing basketball and is a Golden State Warriors fan(*since-2013*).

www.ingramcontent.com/pod-product-compliance
Lightning Source LLC
Chambersburg PA
CBHW040816200526
45159CB00024B/2998